The Canada Jay

The National Bird of Canada?

Canada Jay logo designed by Paul Riss of Round Agency Inc. (weareround.com)

Logo du Mésangeai du Canada créé par Paul Riss – Round Agency Inc. (weareround.com)

THE
CANADA JAY

THE NATIONAL BIRD
OF CANADA?

DAVID BIRD • DAN STRICKLAND • RYAN NORRIS
ALAIN GOULET • AARON KYLIE • MARK NADJIWAN
MICHEL GOSSELIN • COLLEEN ARCHER

hancock house

Cataloguing data available from Library and Archives Canada
978-0-88839-717-1 [paperback]
978-0-88839-772-0 [epub]

PROUDLY PRINTED & BOUND IN CANADA
This book has been printed on
Forest Stewardship Council® certified paper

MIX
Paper from
responsible sources
FSC® C103567

Cover & Title Page Photo: Michael Runtz "Nature by Runtz"
Production & Design: J. Rade & M. Lamont
Editor: D. Martens

We acknowledge the financial support of the Government of Canada through the
Canada Book Fund and the Canada Council for the Arts, and of the Province of British
Columbia through the British Columbia Arts Council and the Book Publishing Tax Credit.

Funded by the Government of Canada / Financé par le gouvernement du Canada | **Canada** | **BRITISH COLUMBIA** | **BRITISH COLUMBIA ARTS COUNCIL** An agency of the Province of British Columbia

*Hancock House gratefully acknowledges the Halkomelem Speaking
Peoples whose unceded, shared and asserted traditional territories our
offices reside upon.*

Published simultaneously in Canada and the United States by

HANCOCK HOUSE PUBLISHERS LTD.
19313 Zero Avenue, Surrey, B.C. Canada V3Z 9R9
#104-4550 Birch Bay-Lynden Rd, Blaine, WA, U.S.A. 98230-9436
(800) 938-1114   Fax (800) 983-2262
www.hancockhouse.com   info@hancockhouse.com

Robert Bateman's 1981 painting of a Canada Jay entitled "Wrangler's Campsite – Gray Jay" (24" x 16", acrylic on board) depicting a bird patiently perched on an embedded wrangler's axe while awaiting some table scraps

Peinture à l'acrylique d'un Mésangeai du Canada, réalisée par Robert Bateman en 1981 et intitulée « Wrangler's Campsite – Gray Jay » (16 × 24 po). Représentation d'un Mésangeai du Canada perché sur une hache de campement et attendant patiemment des restes de table

TABLE OF CONTENTS

Robert Bateman's 1996 painting entitled "Whiskey Jack" (9" x 13" gouache on Mylar)

Peinture de 1996 par Robert Bateman intitulée « Whiskey Jack » (gouache 13 × 9 po sur Mylar)

FOREWORD

From the time I was a teenager and became a serious naturalist, Algonquin Park seemed like a kind of Nirvana. Our family cottage was in Haliburton County south of the park, but the great and mysterious boreal regions started just north of there. It was and is the land of black spruce, moose and ravens and, not so much, white pines, deer and crows (although there is overlap, of course).

In an effort to promote the Canada Jay as our country's national bird, much has been written about it in recent years. One would think that there is little more to say, but that would be wrong. Having delved a little more deeply into the life and habits of this little (compared to owls and geese) bird, which is ubiquitous in the coniferous forests across northern Canada, I am quite amazed at the interesting intricacies of its history and habits. The fact that many First Nations people refer to it as a trickster and camp robber only attests to its ingenuity and adaptability to conditions. It is also from First Nations that its other name, "whiskyjack," is derived.

It is often found nesting in a blizzard, the nest lined with tent caterpillar cocoons, as it withstands below-freezing temperatures—how very Canadian! Unlike many of our birds, the Canada Jay is also refreshingly monogamous, thereby setting a good example to all. Not to mention that its fledglings from previous years are known to help feed the new fledglings in a familial setting. Omnivorous, it spends a great deal of its time diligently caching compacted pellets of food under the bark of spruce trees for future use. Other animals and birds often find these caches, so the Canada Jay unwittingly helps feed other species. As a Canadian, I would be proud to be represented by such a bird!

Like our country, the Canada Jay is a quiet bird but not shy. In fact, it is sociable in a gentle way, which is the way I like to think of us Canadians. You see, all of my experiences with Canada Jays are those that I have had in the wilderness. For me, they are always an experience of joy. What especially appeals to me is that friendly, almost confiding way the Canada jay has with human beings. My first memory of them is seeing one as a teenager in Algonquin Park, as we were driving through the gate in winter. Having spotted a Canada Jay, we stopped the vehicle. Rather than fly away, the bird flew nearer to us! So, on a hunch I took a little piece of sandwich and held it out. At that moment, I was treated to the thrill of the trusting little bird landing on my fingers. Friendly but wild. Could that be Canadians at their best? On another occasion in Algonquin Park, I was eating my lunch. I held a piece of fruitcake in my outstretched hand, and a Canada Jay promptly landed on my fingertips and took the tidbit in its bill. For me, what a thrilling interface that was between the avian world and the human world! A third encounter with equally charming results was on a pack horse trip in the Chilcotins years later. It seems that the social Canada jay is always on the lookout for a picnic.

The distribution map of the Canada Jay is basically the map of Canada, so the Canada Jay, or whiskyjack, is, for all intents and purposes, all ours. While we do share it a bit with our American friends in Alaska and western mountains, it is basically found all over forested Canada, from coast to coast to coast.

While some might think that the Canada Jay looks rather plain in plumage, this bird is intelligent, friendly, tough and courageous. Just like us Canadians, eh?

— **Robert Bateman**

DEDICATION TO THE CANADA JAY

When we were filming caribou in the Yukon some years ago, we made camp in the far northwest corner of the Canadian mainland. Our camp was north of Old Crow, on the Porcupine River, just a few kilometres from the Alaska border. Two Gwich'in guides, father and son, took us there by boat, and shared our camp. It was cold, late fall. The loons had gone south, the snowy owls were on their way, the Canada geese had left—leaving only the tough, truly Canadian species that face winter.

Janet Foster getting some video of her favourite bird (John Foster)

Janet Foster capte sur vidéo son oiseau préféré. (John Foster)

A pair of Canada Jays often perch side by side touching one another (Michael Runtz) | Les membres d'un couple de Mésangeais du Canada se perchent souvent en se touchant (Michael Runtz)

And as we prepared bacon for breakfast over a warming open fire, a pair of Canada Jays came down to inspect the frying pan.

Reflecting on this later, we wondered how many thousands of times this scene must have been repeated throughout the exploration history of Canada, as explorers and their native guides moved across the northern landscape and were welcomed at every campsite by Canada Jays. To us, this was the perfect, historic scenario that speaks to our respect and admiration for this northern bird.

The Canada Jay performs the official greeting for everyone venturing into the Canadian wilderness, and keeps up that tradition to this day, in all seasons.

— **John and Janet Foster,**
famous Canadian wildlife cinematographers

CHAPTER ONE

WHY CANADA NEEDS A NATIONAL BIRD

Birding (aka birdwatching) continues to be one of the fastest growing hobbies in North America. According to one survey, one in five Canadians spends an average of at least 133 days a year watching, monitoring, feeding, filming, or photographing the 450 or so different kinds of birds in our country. That almost doubles the seventy days a year Canadians spend gardening. Birds, being so numerous, so colourful and so diverse, are likely the most common types of wild animals we see on a regular basis. More than a quarter of our households have installed feeders and bird houses in our backyards, and almost ten percent of us have bought bird identification books and binoculars and taken trips specifically to see birds and attend hundreds of bird festivals all over North America. That is big bucks for our economy!

In 2018, hundreds of avid birders from 16 states and five provinces flocked to the tiny Maritime town of Miramichi, N.B., to see the very first Mistle Thrush from northern Europe to visit our shores. In February of that same year, more than 62 percent of the world's 10,000 bird species comprising 27 million individual birds were recorded by 200,000 birdwatchers in over 100 countries during a four-day period, called the Great Backyard Bird Count. No fewer than 14,000 of them were Canadians.

But it's not about the money! Birds do a lot for humans. They eat pests, pollinate our plants and crops, disperse seeds; their eggs and meat (yes, chickens are birds!) feed us and their feathers keep us warm. They have even helped us win wars by teaching our military about flight, camouflage and sentry systems, and acting as vital message carriers. Birds have saved human lives not just by serving as the literal "canary in the coal mine" but also by globally warning us of other environmental health hazards, such as carcinogenic pesticides and industrial byproducts. Sadly, it took the unbelievable, senseless annihilation of literally billions of passenger pigeons on our continent to help promote a burgeoning conservation movement and herald a new era of environmentalism. And today, our birds are warning humans about the direct and indirect impacts of climate warming on our planet.

However, we also celebrate birds because of their intrinsic value. Who can deny that birds entertain us in so many ways with their beauty, their song and their flight? How many great writers, artists, filmmakers, and even aviators and astronauts were inspired by these amazing, unique creatures?! If you ask a birdwatcher what they see in birds, they might respond by saying, "What does one see in the works of Shakespeare, the paintings of Van Gogh, or the music of Mozart?" In short, a world without birds would be not just a biologically diminished world, but also an emotionally diminished one. And if we lose our birds, we will lose ourselves.

Birds can also take credit for uniting nations. In 1789, George Washington became the first President of the United States, and the Bald Eagle became its official bird. The Founding Fathers chose the eagle because of its fierce beauty and proud independence. Americans today revere their Bald Eagle. Drive anywhere in the states and you will see flags and signs depicting the bird. Trained Bald Eagles are often flown at major sporting events such as the Super Bowl, the World Series, and the Indianapolis 500. One bird named Challenger, a 28-year-old rescue bird, has flown to the national anthem at no fewer than 350 public events in the past two decades! In 1970, the United States Postal Service adopted the

The Bald Eagle is the national bird of
the United States (Christian Sasse)

Le Pygargue à tête blanche est
l'oiseau national des États-Unis
(Christian Sasse)

Canada Jays will store food at any time of year, but the behaviour becomes especially conspicuous in the fall (John and Janet Foster)

Les Mésangeais du Canada cachent de la nourriture en tout temps de l'année, mais ce comportement devient particulièrement évident à l'automne. (John et Janet Foster)

"standing Bald Eagle" as its official seal, reflecting the determined and undeniably American spirit of its employees.

The U.S. is not alone in adopting an official bird. No fewer than 106 of the world's 195 countries have official birds, twenty-one of them not official as yet. This includes tiny countries such as Israel (Hoopoe), Honduras (Scarlet Macaw) and Estonia (Barn Swallow). Some other well-known ones are the Kiwi for New Zealand and the Doctor Bird for Jamaica. (I rather like that last choice!)

Canada is not listed in Wikipedia's List of National Birds. Why? Because we do not have one! Yet our country does in fact have national symbols. According to its web site for "Official Symbols of Canada," we learn that the beaver was given official status as an emblem of Canada on March 24, 1975. Its hard-working nature and its role in early commerce that helped make Canada what it is today made it a popular choice. The U.S. chose the North American bison as its official mammal for the same reason. However, our country was also built on forestry and the maple sugar industry, which convinced our government to adopt the maple tree, at least the generic version, as an official symbol in 1996. Watch any Olympics or international athletic contest and one cannot help note that we have two official

The Common Raven is the official bird of the Northwest Territories (Michael Runtz) | Le Grand Corbeau est l'emblème aviaire des Territoires du Nord-Ouest (Michael Runtz)

colours: red and white. That was a result of the proclamation of Canada's coat of arms by King George V way back in 1921. Put those colours and the maple leaf together, and voilà, we have created our Canadian flag, one we adopted in 1965 and one that is easily and respectfully recognized all over the world. How many of us do not get choked up at least a little when we see that flag being raised at major events around the world? Hey, we even have a national horse! A breed all on its own and known for its great strength and endurance, resilience, intelligence and good temper, the Canadian horse was officially declared to be our national breed as recently as May 2002. And every Canadian worth his or her salt knows that ice hockey is *our* game. By passing the National Sports of Canada Act on May 12, 1994, our country officially declared ice hockey as the national winter sport and lacrosse as the national summer sport. Need I say anything about our national anthem?! But no official bird.

The world is full of symbols, whether it be sports uniforms, company logos or even traffic signs. Some societies wear gold rings to symbolize the bond of marriage. Some symbols such as stop signs are highly functional, while others convey nonmaterial, cultural meanings. Some are somewhat trivial, for example blue ribbons or gold medals. But an official bird? It is much more than that. It could not only represent all those wonderful things birds do for us, but also symbolize the very nature of Canadians as being the friendly, hardy and intelligent people that we are seen to be by many folks around the world.

We've got an official mammal, a tree, a horse, and two sports. Why not a bird? Each July 1, we Canadians proudly get together from coast to coast to coast to proclaim our love for our country. What perfect timing for our federal government to officially adopt a national bird! And yes, I know that such things do not take place overnight in government circles and that governments come and go, but a mere announcement of the intent to do so is all that would be needed. Let's get it done!

— **David M. Bird**

CHAPTER TWO

NATIONAL BIRDS OF THE WORLD

List of National Birds (Adapted from Wikipedia, April 6, 2021)

COUNTRY	NAME OF BIRD	SCIENTIFIC NAME
Angola	Red-crested turaco	*Tauraco erythrolophus*
Anguilla	Zenaida dove	*Zenaida aurita*
Antigua and Barbuda	Magnificent frigatebird	*Fregata magnificens*
Argentina	Rufous hornero	*Furnarius rufus*
Aruba	Brown-throated parakeet	*Eupsittula pertinax arubensis*
Australia*	Emu	*Dromaius novaehollandiae*
Austria	Barn swallow	*Hirundo rustica*
Bahamas	American flamingo	*Phoenicopterus ruber*
Bahrain	White-eared bulbul	*Pycnonotus leucotis*
Bangladesh	Oriental magpie-robin	*Copsychus saularis*
Belarus*	White stork	*Ciconia ciconia*

COUNTRY	NAME OF BIRD	SCIENTIFIC NAME
Belgium	Common kestrel	*Falco tinnunculus*
Belize	Keel-billed toucan	*Ramphastos sulfuratus*
Bermuda*	Bermuda petrel	*Pterodroma cahow*
Bhutan	Common raven	*Corvus corax*
Bolivia	Andean condor	*Vultur gryphus*
Botswana	Kori bustard	*Ardeotis kori*
Brazil	Rufous-bellied thrush	*Turdus rufiventris*
British Virgin Islands	Mourning dove	*Zenaida macroura*
Cambodia	Giant ibis	*Thaumatibis gigantea*
Cayman Islands	Grand Cayman parrot	*Amazona leucocephala caymanensis*
Chile	Andean condor	*Vultur gryphus*
China*	Red-crowned crane	*Grus japonensis*
Colombia	Andean condor	*Vultur gryphus*
Costa Rica	Clay-colored thrush	*Turdus grayi*
Croatia*	Common nightingale	*Luscinia megarhynchos*
Cuba	Cuban trogon	*Priotelus temnurus*
Denmark	Mute swan	*Cygnus olor*
Dominica	Imperial amazon	*Amazona imperialis*
Dominican Republic	Palmchat	*Dulus dominicus*
Ecuador	Andean condor	*Vultur gryphus*
El Salvador	Turquoise-browed motmot	*Eumomota superciliosa*
Estonia	Barn swallow	*Hirundo rustica*
Faroe Islands	Eurasian oystercatcher	*Haematopus ostralegus*
Finland*	Whooper swan	*Cygnus cygnus*
France*	Gallic rooster	*Gallus gallus*

COUNTRY	NAME OF BIRD	SCIENTIFIC NAME
Germany*	Golden eagle	*Aquila chrysaetos*
Gibraltar	Barbary partridge	*Alectoris barbara*
Greece*	Little owl	*Athene noctua*
Grenada	Grenada dove	*Leptotila wellsi*
Guatemala	Resplendent quetzal	*Pharomachrus mocinno*
Guyana	Hoatzin	*Opisthocomus hoazin*
Haiti	Hispaniolan trogon	*Priotelus roseigaster*
Honduras	Scarlet macaw	*Ara macao*
Hungary	Saker falcon	*Falco cherrug*
Iceland	Gyrfalcon	*Falco rusticolus*
India	Indian peacock	*Pavo cristatus*
Indonesia	Javan hawk-eagle	*Nisaetus bartelsi*
Iran	Common nightingale	*Luscinia megarhynchos*
Iraq	Chukar partridge	*Alectoris chukar*
Ireland*	Northern lapwing	*Vanellus vanellus*
Israel	Hoopoe	*Upupa epops*
Italy	Italian sparrow	*Passer italiae*
Jamaica	Doctor bird	*Trochilus polytmus*
Japan	Green pheasant	*Phasianus versicolor*
Jordan	Sinai rosefinch	*Carpodacus synoicus*
Kenya*	Lilac-breasted roller	*Coracias caudatus*
Latvia	White wagtail	*Motacilla alba*
Liberia	Garden bulbul	*Pycnonotus barbatus*
Lithuania	White stork	*Ciconia ciconia*
Luxembourg	Goldcrest	*Regulus regulus*
Malta	Blue rock thrush	*Monticola solitarius*
Mexico	Golden eagle	*Aquila chrysaetos*

COUNTRY	NAME OF BIRD	SCIENTIFIC NAME
Mongolia	Saker falcon	*Falco cherrug*
Montserrat	Monserrat oriole	*Icterus oberi*
Myanmar	Grey peacock-pheasant	*Polyplectron bicalcaratum*
Namibia	African fish eagle	*Haliaeetus vocifer*
Nepal	Himalayan monal	*Lophophorus impejanus*
Netherlands*	Black-tailed godwit	*Limosa limosa*
New Zealand*	Kiwi	*Apteryx mantelli*
Nicaragua	Turquoise-browed motmot	*Eumomota superciliosa*
Nigeria	Black-crowned crane	*Balearica pavonina*
North Korea	Northern goshawk	*Accipiter gentilis*
Norway	White-throated dipper	*Cinclus cinclus*
Pakistan	Chukar partridge	*Alectoris chukar*
Palestine*	Palestine sunbird	*Cinnyris oseus*
Panama	Harpy eagle	*Harpia harpyja*
Papua New Guinea	Raggania bird-of-paradise	*Paradisaea raggiana*
Paraguay	Bare-throated bellbird	*Procnias nudicollis*
Peru	Andean cock-of-the-rock	*Rupicola peruvianus*
Philippines	Philippine eagle	*Pithecophaga jefferyi*
Poland	White-tailed eagle	*Haliaeetus albicilla*
Puerto Rico	Puerto Rican spindalis	*Spindalis portoricensis*
Saint Helena	Saint Helena plover	*Charadrius sanctaehelenae*
Saint Kitts and Nevis	Brown pelican	*Pelecanus occidentalis*
Saint Vincent and the Grenadines	St Vincent parrot	*Amazona guildingii*
Scotland*	Golden eagle	*Aquila chrysaetos*

COUNTRY	NAME OF BIRD	SCIENTIFIC NAME
Serbia	Griffon vulture (also Eagle)	*Gyps fulvus*
Singapore*	Crimson sunbird	*Aethopyga siparaja*
South Africa	Blue crane	*Anthropoides paradisea*
Sri Lanka	Sri Lanka junglefowl	*Gallus lafayetii*
Swaziland	Purple-crested turaco	*Tauraco porphyreolophus*
Sweden	Common blackbird	*Turdus merula*
Thailand	Siamese fireback	*Lophura diardi*
Trinidad**	Scarlet ibis	*Eudocimus ruber*
Tobago**	Cocrico	*Ortalis ruficauda*
Uganda	East African crowned crane	*Balearica regulorum gibbericeps*
Ukraine*	White stork	*Ciconia ciconia*
United Arab Emirates	Falcon	*Falco sp.*
United Kingdom*	European robin	*Erithacus rubecula*
United States	Bald eagle	*Haliaeetus leucocephalus*
Uruguay*	Southern lapwing	*Vanellus chilensis*
Venezuela	Venezuelan troupial	*Icterus icterus*
Wales*	Red kite	*Milvus milvus*
Zambia	African fish eagle	*Haliaeetus vocifer*
Zimbabwe	African fish eagle	*Haliaeetus vocifer*

* Unofficial
** Same country but two national birds

The Great Horned Owl is the official bird of Alberta (Michael Runtz)

Le Grand-duc d'Amérique est l'emblème aviaire de l'Alberta (Michael Runtz)

CHAPTER THREE

A WHIMSICAL LOOK AT THE OFFICIAL BIRDS OF CANADA'S PROVINCES AND TERRITORIES

ALBERTA: *Great Horned Owl*
While large ear tufts are major features,
At night it's hard to see these creatures.
When courting they all give a hoot;
Prospective mates must find that cute.
As hunters they are highly rated
And in the past were loved or hated.

BRITISH COLUMBIA: *Steller's Jay*
These crested birds with tastes eclectic
Have natures that might seem electric.
Their raucous calls can often grate,
But they sing sweetly to their mate.
Coniferous forests in the west
Are habitats they like the best.

MANITOBA: *Great Gray Owl*

The Great Gray Owl's facial disc
Puts rodents at the highest risk
Since funneled sounds mean Grays can hear
The slightest noises far and near.
As birds deserving of their name,
They're graceful fliers, and quite tame.

NEW BRUNSWICK: *Black-Capped Chickadee*

Black Caps always wear a crown,
Their mating call is up, then down;
They're famous for their repartee,
Like cheery *Chick-a-dee-dee-dee*.
As acrobats they are renowned,
And some of them stay north year-round.

NEWFOUNDLAND AND LABRADOR: *Atlantic Puffin*

In Newfoundland and Labrador
The Puffin seeks a coastal shore
And thinks that islands are the best
When scraping out a soft turf nest.
At other times the place to be
Is diving in the open sea.

NORTHWEST TERRITORIES: *Gyrfalcon*

Earth's largest falcons use harsh words
And often dine on other birds.
They're speedy, so they also prey
On Arctic hares that pass their way.
While hunting they might be in luck
And meet a not-so-lucky duck.

The Atlantic Puffin is the official bird of
Newfoundland and Labrador (Michael Runtz)

Le Macareux moine est l'emblème aviaire de
Terre-Neuve-et-Labrador (Michael Runtz)

NOVA SCOTIA: *Osprey*
These "fish hawks" surely know refraction
When hunting with precision action,
Their call is an ascending whistle,
They dive just like a guided missile.
Those spines on toes hold slippery prey
So captured fish can't get away.

NUNAVUT: *Rock Ptarmigan*
Remarkably this tough grouse copes
Atop bleak tundra's barren slopes.
With feathered feet they come and go
And walk with ease on deepest snow.
Their camouflage is winter white
And mottled brown in summer's light.

ONTARIO: *Common Loon*
Yodels, hoots, or crazy laughter
Tell us what each Loon is after.
Rear-placed legs make walks no breeze,
But dense bones mean they dive with ease.
Small bass, sunfish, pike and perch
Are fair game for this hunter's search.

PRINCE EDWARD ISLAND: *Blue Jay*
Brazen, boisterous and bold,
This impish bird's quite tame, we're told.
"Jay! Jay! Jay!" are favourite words,
Plus mimicry of other birds.
With necklace, tail bars and a crest,
The Blue Jay always looks its best.

QUEBEC: *Snowy Owl*

These Arctic owls are snowy white
Though youngsters are not quite as light.
They're lemming lovers with a wish
To catch one as their favourite dish.
They'll perch on fences or on posts
And swoop from those like silent ghosts.

SASKATCHEWAN: *Sharp-Tailed Grouse*

In summer these grouse like the ground,
In winter up in trees they're found.
Their pointed tails are edged with white
Quite visible when they're in flight.
When it's time for wildly wooing
The males all dance and do some cooing.

YUKON: *Common Raven*

These clever birds are black as night,
Their coarse-croak call can cause a fright.
They post a guard while they are feeding,
They're loyal mates when they are breeding.
Some say this bird's an evil sign,
But others see it as divine.

CANADA: *Canada Jay?*

These smart birds found throughout the land
Will come and eat right from your hand.
Sometimes called a campground robber,
They cover food with preserving slobber,
Then store as much as they can stash
And dine in winter on their cache.

— **Colleen Rutherford Archer**

With a face like that, it is hard to argue that Canada Jays are not cute! (Marcel Gahbauer)

Avec une telle frimousse, qui pourrait dire que le Mésangeai du Canada n'est pas mignon? (Marcel Gahbauer)

CHAPTER FOUR

WHY THE CANADA JAY SHOULD BE CANADA'S NATIONAL BIRD!

I n no order of importance, here are no fewer than **eighteen** reasons (some arguably more laudable than others) why the Canada Jay would be a great choice for the national bird of Canada. It is:

1) Found in all thirteen provinces and territories;
2) A member of the jay and crow family, arguably the smartest birds on the planet;
3) Not an official bird species for any of the ten provinces and recognized territories nor any other country;
4) Very hardy, like all Canadians, having highly adapted to living in very cold regions and nesting in temperatures of -30 C;
5) A year-round resident, i.e. not a "snowbird" like the Common Loon;
6) A bird with strong cultural significance for many of Canada's First Nations. The widely used name, "whisky-jack," is derived from one of the Canada Jay's names in the Algonquian family of languages, quite likely wîskicâhk, one of the words used in Cree. "Whiskyjack" is one of

very few English vernacular names for a Canadian bird species borrowed from an indigenous language, and the only one in common use today;

7) The first bird, and perhaps the only bird, to greet thousands of explorers, fur trappers, prospectors, settlers, and First Nations folk, around their campfires in the dead of chilly Canadian winters;

8) Not an endangered species, and thus not at a serious risk of disappearing;

9) A bird that figures prominently in the boreal forest ecological zone, constituting a vast and distinctive part of our country;

10) Not a hunted species, so not shot by Canadians;

11) Like all Canadians, extremely friendly toward humans and conspicuous residents of our national and provincial parks from coast to coast;

12) A species that could not have a better name for the national bird, as it is now, once again, officially called the Canada Jay in English (and "mésangeai du Canada" in French).

13) Not regarded as an obnoxious or nuisance species;

14) Not likely to be confused with any other bird species;

15) Not a circumpolar species, i.e. not found in other northern countries (as is the Snowy Owl);

16) Not flamboyantly coloured and so easily reproducible in logo format;

17) Not a common backyard feeder bird and thus, will hopefully force Canadians to get out into nature and to enjoy and appreciate our extensive boreal forests and our great parks, and at the same time, improving one's health and well-being;

18) The official logo bird of the historic International Ornithological Congress in Ottawa in 1986; it was "the most Canadian bird" they could find!

— **David M. Bird**

CHAPTER FIVE

THE NATIONAL BIRD PROJECT

"There are a lot of great birds to choose from for Canada's national bird, but have you considered the puffin? It's a pretty cool bird. It can walk. It can fly some. It's a friendly bird. Puffins ... pick 'em!" So went the twenty-four-second *This Hour Has 22 Minutes* "Puffins Attack Ad" in an early February 2015 episode. (There were also attack ads for the Common Loon and Canada Goose in the same episode.)

At *Canadian Geographic* magazine, where I am the editor-in-chief, we were stunned by the national comedy television institution's spoofing of our National Bird Project, which we'd launched just a month earlier in our January/February issue, in an effort to rectify, by the country's sesquicentennial in 2017, Canada's lack of an official avian emblem.

They say imitation is the highest form of flattery, but as the episode aired and helped amplify our initiative, we sure felt being parodied might indeed be the highest of compliments. And as you might imagine, one of the many things the National Bird Project lent itself to was puns, and the *22 Minutes* spots certainly helped our plan take flight.

Of course, the seeds for the project originally emerged in mid-2014. Tyrone Burke, a longtime contributor to the magazine, had observed to publisher Gilles Gagnier that while Canada has a national arboreal emblem (the maple tree), a national horse (the Canadian), two national sports (lacrosse and hockey) and a national mammal (the beaver), it did not have a national bird. When the idea was shared with me, I immediately saw an opportunity (although at the time, I could not have imagined the heights it would fly to): if *Time* could annually name a person of the year, and *People* could determine the planet's sexiest man every year, why couldn't *Canadian Geographic* name a national bird?

And with the country about to celebrate that aforementioned milestone birthday just a couple of years from that time, we figured we'd help give the nation an appropriate (and long overdue) gift. So, we set the wheels in motion to help proclaim an official bird for the country, kicking off our National Bird Project in that January/February 2015 edition. In it, four prominent Canadian writers penned essays opining what the bird should be—Will Ferguson promoted the Canada Goose, Alissa York vied for the Great Gray Owl, Charlotte Grey opted for the Osprey and Noah Richler pushed for the Common Raven.

The intent of the essays was to inspire our readers' participation, and we pointed them to an accompanying website (nationalbird. canadiangeographic.ca) where they (and fellow Canadians) could vote for their favourite species and submit their own 300-word essays on which bird should represent the country. To help make that task a little easier, we solicited the help of Bird Studies Canada (now Birds Canada), a national nonprofit organization dedicated to conserving wild birds through sound science, on-the-ground actions, innovative partnerships, public engagement and science-based advocacy.

Working with Jody Allair, director of citizen science and community engagement at Birds Canada, our managing editor, Nick Walker, created a short-list of fifty species, including songbirds, upland and game birds, wading birds, gulls and shorebirds, woodpeckers

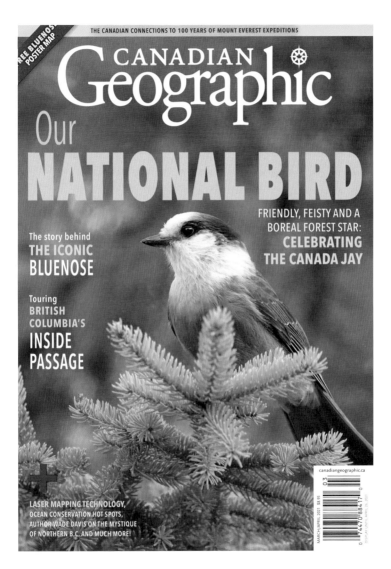

The March 25, 2021 cover of Canadian Geographic magazine reminds Canadians that the Canada Jay is a most fitting choice to be our national bird, but we still need the federal government to officially recognize it

Le 25 mars 2021, la couverture du magazine Canadian Geographic rappelait aux Canadiens que le Mésangeai du Canada est le meilleur choix comme oiseau national, mais nous avons encore besoin de la reconnaissance officielle du gouvernement fédéral

The Snowy Owl is the official bird of Quebec (Michael Runtz)

Le Harfang des neige est l'emblème aviaire du Québec (Michael Runtz)

and hummingbirds, loons, waterfowl and seabirds, and raptors, that were felt likely to be the most popular options. But we also gave voters the option to share write-in candidates. Over the course of the project, while we got a few serious suggestions, we also got a number of fun recommendations: a beaver on a hang glider, the Manitoba mosquito, snowbirds, Big Bird, Rusty the Rooster from *The Friendly Giant*, St-Hubert's rotisserie chicken and Birdy McBirdface.

Ultimately, we promised to proclaim a winner based on the public's vote in the magazine's November/December 2016 issue, such that the federal government could follow our lead and name an official bird in time for the big bash on July 1, 2017.

That was the plan. Then that *22 Minutes* episode with the attack ads aired and our flight path changed—because we simply hadn't anticipated how eagerly Canadians well beyond our 4.1 million monthly readers would flock to our initiative. Other national media outlets began calling and doing stories—*The Globe and Mail*, *National Post*, CBC's *The National*, and radio stations big and small across the country. And the votes started flooding into our website—at such a rate that, during one day that spring, following a flurry of news coverage, it crashed, forcing an upgrade.

And the website wasn't just getting tens of thousands of votes, it was getting almost the same number of thoughtful, lengthy, impassioned arguments for favoured species, each one posted to the site and available for all voters to review. One day in the early going we got a submission from a Robert Bateman. Not *the* Robert Bateman, we thought? But, yes, the renowned Canadian wildlife artist had filled out the form on our website announcing his vote for the "friendly but wild" gray jay.

Of course, it wasn't the first of the votes from a prominent Canadian for the hardy, gregarious bird also known as the whiskey jack, which was quickly gaining momentum as what seemed to us at the magazine at the time a dark-horse candidate for the title. David M. Bird, the coordinating editor of this publication and emeritus professor of ornithology at Montreal's McGill University, contributed a compelling list of over a dozen reasons (now expanded to Eighteen – see Chapter 4) why the Gray Jay would be a great choice. Bird would go on to launch his own independent campaign vying for the species.

Meanwhile, at the magazine, managing the National Bird Project became a job in and of itself—answering regular media inquiries, approving website comment submissions, managing the tens of thousands of votes coming in and editing a series of essays for each issue of our magazine through 2015 and into 2016 from well-known Canadians promoting a bird of their choice, each accompanied by an amazing illustration by Toronto-based artist Charlene Chua. And as mid-2016 approached, we were seemingly suddenly confronted with the realities of figuring out how to name a national bird, with what had become apparent was worth far greater consideration than just the tally of a popularity contest (and wanting to learn from the mistakes made by the UK's Natural Environment Research Council, whose online ship-naming poll led to the moniker *Boaty McBoatface*).

As summer 2016 began, it was clear that five birds had emerged as leading candidates for the honour: the Common Loon, the Snowy Owl, the Canada Goose and the Black-capped Chickadee (my personal favourite, lest you think I am/was biased!), with the Gray Jay solidly in third place, each receiving significantly higher numbers of votes than any other bird. So, we announced an originally unplanned second phase of the competition: a new round of voting among the final five, a live Can Geo Talks event "debate" at Ottawa's Canadian Museum of Nature—where then Environment and Climate Change Minister Catherine McKenna provided opening remarks (watch the entire debate on YouTube, it was great fun!)—and consultations with leading cultural and birding experts. The combination of these would inform our final decision. (Memorably, at the debate ornithologist David Bird, arguing in favour of the Gray Jay, made a dramatic statement noting that when Canada adopted the Maple Leaf as its flag in 1965 it didn't simply elevate the flag of Ontario or Quebec, but rather

The Black-capped Chickadee is the official bird of New Brunswick (Michael Runtz)

La Mésange à tête noire est l'emblème aviaire du Nouveau-Brunswick (Michael Runtz)

chose an emblem that was "fresh and new." That point was met with unsolicited applause from the audience.)

The unplanned change in process led to another significant round of mass media coverage — and a sprint to the finish. You can read the explanations of others here about why the Gray Jay was ultimately chosen (and since restored to "Canada Jay", we humbly believe in no small part thanks to our competition), but our deliberations ultimately agreed. That bird met all our reasonable criteria best: found in every province and territory, but not already one of their official birds; and important to Indigenous Peoples. Publisher Gilles Gagnier revealed *Canadian Geographic*'s selection—the cover subject of our December 2016 issue "Our New National Bird, The Gray Jay"—at The Royal Canadian Geographical Society's College of Fellows Annual Dinner on Nov. 16, 2016.

I spent the following days speaking to media in Canada and around the world, including CBC, the *Toronto Star*, BBC.com, slate. com, *The Globe and Mail*, CTV news and many more. During the course of the project, its hashtag (#CanadaBird) trended number one on Twitter multiple times, and to this day, we see and hear individuals and groups referring to the Gray Jay (especially with its now-restored, original official name, Canada Jay*) as our country's national bird—despite the fact the federal government has yet to officially recognize it as such.

But the greatest compliment? On its Nov. 24, 2016, episode, the *22 Minutes* crew once again spoofed the National Bird Project and our final choice of the Gray (Canada) Jay. Said comedian Cathy Jones: "I'm not a fan. There's hardly any meat on it. Now a loon, on the other hand, that's good eating."

— **Aaron Kylie**

CHAPTER SIX

WHY THE VERY NEAT GRAY (CANADA) JAY BEAT OUT THE VERY COMMON LOON

On November 16, 2016, at their College of Fellows Annual Dinner in the Canadian War Museum, the Royal Canadian Geographical Society (RCGS) stunned many Canadians (and some folks elsewhere in the world, too!) by choosing the third-place Canada Jay over the first-place Common Loon as their candidate to be Canada's national bird. While many Canucks across the country were happy with this choice, many were not, particularly those who believe in the democratic process, i.e. the most votes win, and also the many folks who voted for the iconic Common Loon. More details on the RCGS's National Bird Project by Aaron Kylie are available in Chapter 5, but here is the short version as to why the Common Loon was not chosen as the best candidate for Canada's national bird.

This wonderful political cartoon by Gilles Lamontagne first appeared in the Ottawa Citizen on November 18, 2016, well before the original official name, Canada Jay, was officially restored in July 2018. (*Gilles Lamontagne lamontagneart.com*)

Cette caricature politique par Gilles Lamontagne est parue pour la première fois dans l'Ottawa Citizen du 18 novembre 2016, avant que le nom Canada Jay ne soit officiellement rétabli en juillet 2018. (*Gilles Lamontagne, lamontagneart.com*)

First, let's dispel the argument that due democratic process was not adhered to. In January 2015, the RCGS asked Canadians to *help* them choose a bird species that could best represent our broad nation, composed of a variety of habitats. The idea of the poll was simply to encourage debate among Canadians about the need for a national bird, to present a slate of potential candidates for a vote, to stimulate the writing of essays championing various species, and finally, to consult with bird experts across the country to make the most meaningful choice. There was never any intent to merely make it a popularity contest by choosing the bird that won the popular vote. After all, what if the iconic fourth-place Canada goose had won with the most votes? Can you imagine the outrage from coast to coast!

When the poll closed on Aug. 31, 2016, roughly 50,000 Canadians had cast their votes. The five finalists, in order, were the Common

Loon, Snowy Owl, Gray jay (now Canada Jay), Canada Goose, and Black-capped Chickadee. On Sept. 19, the RCGS entered the second phase of the process by convening a panel of experts in Ottawa to publicly debate which of the five species they believed to be most worthy of this honour. Judging by the applause and cheering that night, Team Gray Jay won the debate. Next, the RCGS consulted with a number of bird experts to make a final choice among the five finalists, created an issue of *Canadian Geographic* to explain their decision, and announced it at their Fellows Dinner. And then the loon poop hit the fan.

So why the Canada Jay, you ask? Here is an expanded discussion of some of the main reasons listed by me in Chapter Four.

First and most important, this little bird is found in every province and territory in Canada. Essentially, its distribution map practically mirrors the borders of our country with some minor exceptions, i.e. the Pacific Northwest of the continent and bordering states including Alaska. The Canada Jay does not exist in any other country in the world. Nor can it be confused with any other bird. For example, for those Common Raven fans out there, 99.5 percent of Canadians cannot tell the difference between that species and an American Crow! Moreover, unlike the other four finalists, the Canada Jay does not—I repeat, does not—leave our country in our winter months. More on that later.

Next, and this is an extremely important consideration, the Canada Jay has not already been claimed as an official bird for any other geographical entity, unlike its competitors. The Common Loon has been Ontario's official bird for eons (and Minnesota's!), the Snowy Owl is Quebec's bird, and the Black-capped Chickadee is the official bird for New Brunswick, Maine and Massachusetts, As for the Canada Goose, its exploding numbers and unfortunate habit of coating lawns and golf courses with layers of poop makes it a non-starter for any political entity. Look at it this way: when we selected our Canadian flag on Feb. 15, 1965, we did not elevate the flags of Ontario, Quebec or New Brunswick to national status.

We chose something "fresh and new," a flag that all Canadians are so proud of today.

As for the character and quality of the Canada Jay, you could not find a more Canadian bird. First, as a member of the corvid family (crows, ravens, magpies and jays), it is one of the smartest birds on the planet. Its brain-to-body ratio is equivalent to that of the chimpanzee and dolphin and nearly rivals that of the human. Second, the Canada Jay is extremely tough and hardy. By not leaving the country in winter, it has adapted itself to not only surviving our harsh Canadian winters but breeding then as well. This bird is known to incubate its eggs at -30 Celsius! Third, Canada Jays are extremely friendly, readily coming down to perch on open hands, even without food, and on ski poles, cameras and spotting scopes, without any training whatsoever. Fourth, unlike many songbirds in the world, Canada Jays are not promiscuous and the mates do not cheat on each other. The pair remains together year-round, often flying together everywhere and even perching side by side, touching each other. So, we've got "smart," "hardy," "friendly" and "loyal." What better way to describe the typical Canadian, eh?

It gets better. For almost 150 years, this jay was known as the Canada Jay, but in 1957, for reasons way too complicated to get into here, the American Ornithologists' Union (AOU) decided to rename it the Gray Jay and added insult to injury by adopting the American spelling. Dan Strickland, arguably Canada's foremost expert on the species, to the rescue! After painstaking research on the subject, Dan put together a proposal to restore the original official name and, along with five collaborators and the Society of Canadian Ornithologists, submitted it to the naming committee of the AOU (since renamed the American Ornithological Society). Almost unanimously, the committee members agreed and restored the name! Can you imagine a better name for the national bird of Canada?! But perhaps most Canadians know this bird best as "whiskyjack", a colloquial, anglicized version of an Algonquian (Cree) name, "*wîskicâhk*".

While it is true that the Canada Jay does have what I consider to be the cheeky, cute habit of pilfering food from campers and hikers—hence the occasionally used label "campground robber"—one can also construe this behaviour as simply a clever, opportunistic means of survival. The Canada Jay is also a safe choice for the national bird of Canada. It is neither hunted nor killed as a nuisance species. It is also not endangered and not likely to disappear any time soon, the way the Bald Eagle almost did.

I have saved the best for last. The day after the announcement, many grumpy Canadians were scratching their heads wondering, "What in the heck is this bird?" or "Why don't we pick a bird that I see in my backyard!" Well, the Canada Jay is a denizen of our boreal forest that extends from coast to coast. It is commonly found at ski resorts and in many of our national and provincial parks. In short, to meet our hopeful national birds, Canadians are

The Common Loon is the official bird of Ontario (Michael Runtz) | Le Plongeon huard est l'emblème aviaire de l'Ontario (Michael Runtz)

going to have to get off their duffs and venture outdoors to visit those places to hike, camp, and/or ski. I hope that, during your visit, this marvellous and iconic Canadian bird will come down to greet you, just as it did for millennia, welcoming around their campfires the people who built our nation—the indigenous peoples of Canada and the explorers, trappers and settlers who followed.

Can you really think of a more Canadian bird than the Canada Jay?

— David M. Bird

A Canada Jay gathering cattail down to line its nest (Michael Runtz)

Un Mésangeai du Canada ramassant du duvet de quenouille pour tapisser son nid (Michael Runtz)

CHAPTER SEVEN

THE CANADA JAY—OUR COUNTRY'S REALLY COOL ECOLOGICAL WONDER OF WONDERS!

W henever we speak to audiences about our studies of the Canada Jay, someone almost always comes up afterwards and relates how delighted and astonished they were as a child to have a wild bird actually land on their hand—and sometimes even give a note of disapproval if the hand turned out to be empty! We enjoy hearing about such experiences and are happy to share our own stories about interactions with Canada Jays, along with what we have learned about their behaviour and ecology.

We have had the pleasure and privilege of studying Canada Jays for a combined total of more than sixty-five years. Most of our efforts have been directed at trying to answer questions about a life history that seems to defy all common sense. Questions like: "How do Canada Jays succeed in living on permanent territories right through a boreal forest winter, when other boreal birds have to search far and wide for food—or hightail it for Costa Rica?" Or "How can Canada Jays get away with nesting in winter, and why don't they nest in the late spring or early summer, when conditions are obviously much more favourable?" We don't have answers to all our questions about Canada Jays and their lifestyle—but here are some of the highlights.

Food storage is key. Canada Jays live year-round in the boreal and subalpine forests of Canada, from British Columbia and Yukon in the west, to Newfoundland and Labrador in the east, and north up to the tree line. The reason they can do this, instead of migrating south like most other Canadian birds, is that, ahead of time, in summer and fall, they store the food that allows them to survive the coming winter. Many other members of the crow and jay family store food as well, but Canada Jays do a few things that are extra special. One is that they don't cache food items in the ground, the way other jays do. Instead, they coat their food items with copious, sticky saliva from extra-large salivary glands and then fasten those items well above ground, up in the trees. There, at least in principle, the stored food will remain accessible to jays even when, for months on end, deep snow covers the forest floor. Preparing for this, during a single midsummer day, individual Canada Jays have been seen to make as many as a thousand individual caches—under tufts of lichen, in broken-off branches, and up under the shingle-like scales of bark on the trunks of spruce trees. By the time winter begins, a Canada Jay may have hidden away literally tens of thousands of food items scattered over its territory.

Perish the rot thought! A second unique feature of Canada Jay food storage concerns the kinds of food they store. Other food-storing birds cache nonperishable, long-lasting seeds, but Canada Jays store highly perishable, rot-prone berries, mushrooms, insects and spiders, or bits of vertebrate flesh. The problem is that, if stored food is going to be of use to a jay in the winter, the food has to survive in a jay-friendly form (that is, not in complete decay) between the time the jay stores it in the summer all the way through to the onset of winter. (After that, cold temperatures should ensure the food item's further preservation.) Summers tend to

Canada Jays cache thousands of food items under loose bark and other hidden location but always above the snow line for retrieval during the winter. (Michael Runtz)

Les Mésangeais du Canada dissimulent des milliers de parcelles de nourriture sous l'écorce disloquée et en d'autres endroits bien cachés, mais toujours au-dessus du niveau de la neige afin de pouvoir les récupérer en hiver. (Michael Runtz)

be cooler in the boreal forest, of course, but it turns out that something beyond low temperatures helps to slow down the decay of perishable food stored by Canada Jays in our northern forests. Coniferous trees, particularly various species of spruce, have volatile resins that serve to dissuade or sicken animals that might otherwise want to eat their bark or foliage. Those resins also slow down the action of bacteria and fungi that cause decay. And sure enough, we were able to demonstrate experimentally that perishable food items stored over a summer in contact with the bark of spruce trees decayed much less than when stored in contact with the bark of deciduous trees. So, it seems that Canada Jays, by storing their food in spruce and other conifers, increase the chances that seemingly perishable food items will actually last until the arrival of cold temperatures and therefore help the jays survive through the ensuing winter. How cool is that!

Now, where did I put that blueberry anyway? But even that doesn't explain the whole story. It's all very well if a Canada Jay has stored thousands of food items by the time winter comes around. But then the jay has the little problem of having to find them again. "Little" problem, did we say? Good grief! Can you imagine trying to find a hidden blueberry in the three-dimensional complexity of even a single spruce tree!! And then try to imagine scaling up the problem to all the spruce trees on an entire hundred-hectare (250 acres) jay territory. In fact, there is no doubt that Canada Jays really do find their scattered hidden food stores and, as our research has shown, they do it so successfully that they actually have a higher survival rate in winter than they do in summer. What's more—and this is the real kicker—there is considerable evidence that they find those food items (yes, thousands of food items) by actually remembering them. So, while you don't have to tremble

It is astounding to realize that the Canada Jay can incubate its eggs at temperatures of -30 degrees and then successfully raise the chicks in a snowy, apparently foodless boreal landscape! (Dan Strickland)

Que le Mésangeai du Canada puisse incuber ses œufs à une température aussi froide que -30° C et réussir à élever ses oisillons dans un environnement boréal enneigé sans ressources apparentes, voilà qui est impressionnant! (Dan Strickland)

or go all rubber-kneed the next time a Canada Jay lands on your hand, please realize all the same that you are in the presence of a superior being. Compared to a Canada Jay's memory, yours is a joke.

A nesting most perplexing. One of the Canada Jay's most perplexing behaviours is its late-winter nesting. Pairs often start building their nests in February; eggs are laid in March, then hatch in early April, and the young leave the nest late in that month or in early May. During most of that time the ground is still snow-covered, the lakes are still frozen, and there is no obvious food available to feed to nestlings. By any reasonable standard it is still winter in Canada Jay country and, as if to emphasize that fact, even when Canada Jays are done nesting, the great majority of other bird species still haven't even returned from the south, let alone begun nesting themselves. And yet, in spite of the seemingly adverse conditions, Canada Jays have a very high nesting success rate. You would be correct in surmising that stored food is the key ingredient that allows this impressive performance. However, the question still remains as to why the jays nest in March–April when they could just as easily wait until June and nest when fresh food is abundant, just like almost all other birds in the boreal forest.

It is a fundamental principle in biology that any animal should have a breeding season timed to coincide with the period of maximum availability of food for its young. A genetic strain that does this (call it strain A) will produce more surviving young than other possible strains (B, C, D, etc.) of the same species that reproduce at other, less favourable times of the year. Over time, strain A will come to predominate in the population or even become the only surviving strain, all at the expense of the other less-productive strains—that's how evolution works. But can we believe that Canada Jays that reproduce in the late winter are actually nesting when food for their nestlings is most abundant? It seems doubtful, and when we have provided extra food to nesting adults in winter they have responded by producing more young than normal and young that were in better condition. This strongly suggests that nesting in Canada Jays is *not* timed to coincide with the period of maximum food abundance for their nestlings.

So, does this mean we have stumbled onto a disproof of evolutionary theory? It might seem that way, but the answer is actually no, because it turns out that there are other benefits from early nesting in terms of improved production and development of young — benefits that would not be available from a later nesting. Among other things, early nesters are more likely to escape nest predators like squirrels and migratory hawks; their young are more likely to prevail in competition with later-produced young; and, with nesting out of the way relatively early, both young and old jays have more time to store food for the winter. Being able to store enough food before resources dwindle in the fall is a lot to ask of a Canada Jay that has only just recently flown from its nest. But the food it lays away in its first summer and fall will be the key to surviving a young jay's first winter. It follows, then, that by raising their babies as early as possible, Canada Jay parents give their young the longest possible time to lay in those vital winter supplies and therefore give them their best chance in life. Long live strain A!

Danger, too, shapes Canada Jay behavior. It would be hard to overstate the overwhelming importance of food storage in the life, ecology, and even the social organization of the Canada Jay. But other forces are very important to the Canada Jay as well. For example, the deadly threat posed by Northern Goshawks and other bird-eating raptors in the coastal mountains of British Columbia and the value of having many eyes watching for danger may explain why individuals of the western race of Canada Jays typically live in territorial flocks of up to ten or even more birds, sometimes including two or three mated pairs (not just one).

In the main Canada Jay race that lives in the rest of Canada, territories are rarely occupied by more than three birds: a mated pair and, at most, a single extra, usually one of their own young from the previous nesting. But those birds have a threat of their own to contend with, namely Red Squirrels. Almost all Canada Jay nests are inevitably located inside the territory of an individual squirrel. Even a trio of

One of these four Canada Jay fledglings (in their sooty grey juvenile plumage) will soon expel its siblings from the home territory and it alone will stay with its parents for its first year of life (John and Janet Foster) | Un de ces quatre jeunes Mésangeais du Canada (en plumage juvénile gris-cendré) expulsera bientôt ses frères et sœurs du territoire familial et restera seul avec ses parents pendant la première année de sa vie. (John et Janet Foster)

Canada Jays can do very little against a Red Squirrel determined to make a meal of jay eggs or nestlings, and it isn't surprising, therefore, that nesting jays have evolved behaviour to minimize the chance that a squirrel will discover their nest during the 42–44 days between the laying of the first egg and the final departure of the nestlings from the nest. Jay parents do this chiefly through minimizing the frequency of their feeding visits to the nest—visits that might otherwise betray the locations of the nest to the local squirrel. And they compensate for this reduction by cramming as much food as possible into their expandable throats, thereby maximizing the amount of food brought to the nestlings on each trip. They also have another way to minimize traffic to the nest that could tip off the local squirrel. If a nesting pair of jays is still accompanied by a young bird from the year before, the pair is quite ruthless about preventing it from approaching the nest, even though that extra bird could be helping to provision the nestlings—and in late winter at that, when nesting Canada Jays could seemingly use all the help they could get. But apparently the risk of having their teenager betray the nest location is just too great, and jay parents don't let down their guard until their nestlings become airworthy. At that point, the nestlings depart from the nest and become much less vulnerable to a squirrel attack. Only then do the parents relax their former vigilance against the teenager. With their young safely out of the nest, the adults can start bringing food for them at a higher frequency (with smaller food loads) and they can also permit their young from the year before to help feed the new fledglings. Isn't it amazing that Canada Jays can respond to the dangers they face in such sophisticated ways?

Big trouble when the freezer breaks down. Canada Jays have had to contend with predators for hundreds of thousands of years, but a new threat is looming against which it will be much more difficult to evolve a defense, assuming that is even possible. We noted earlier that the secret sauce of the Canada Jay lifestyle is the ability of the jays to store and later recover thousands of perishable food items. While volatile resins of spruce and other conifers can slow down the bacterial and fungal decay of such food items, the Canada Jay food-storage strategy also relies on cool boreal summer and fall temperatures. It's as if Canada Jays store their food in a fridge, which then, with the arrival of winter temperatures, turns into a full-fledged freezer. The trouble is that climate change is now bringing increasingly warmer falls and winters to Canada Jay country, and that, as far as a Canada Jay is concerned, is bringing increasingly common and widespread fridge and freezer failures. One would expect that the threat to Canada Jays would be most severe at the southern, already warmest edge of their range, and in fact that is what we do see. Since the 1970s, in our main study area in Algonquin Park, Ontario, the number of occupied territories has slowly declined by approximately two-thirds. The

A delighted Evelyn Norris with her favourite Canada Jay in Algonquin Park, Ontario (Amy Newman)

Evelyn Norris, toute ravie avec son Mésangeai du Canada préféré, dans le parc Algonquin, en Ontario. (Amy Newman)

adults seem to survive as well as they ever have, so it's not a question of them starving to death in winter. Instead, the decline seems to be caused by a decrease in the number and possibly the quality of young birds that are available to fill the vacancies left by the eventual deaths of older breeders. Moreover, the decline in breeding productivity is correlated with increases in winter temperatures and with the number of freeze-thaw events. Both such increases would be expected to lower the quantity and nutritional quality of any stored perishable food remaining on a jay territory at the end of winter—food used, at least in part, to feed jay nestlings. Environment Canada, we have a problem. Could you send in the freezer repair man?

The coolest thing of all about Canada Jay behaviour? We said at the outset of this essay that we have had the extraordinary privilege of being able to answer some of the questions about these amazing birds. But many questions remain, and, by way of example, we would like to leave you with one that has been put to us many times: Why are Canada Jays so tame? The fact is we don't know—at least not for sure. That's right; even after decades of trying to learn everything possible about Canada Jays, neither of us has a totally convincing explanation for why they are so trusting. Not that we are complaining. On the contrary, we find this trait of the jays to be totally cool and consider ourselves exceedingly lucky that Canada Jays are the way they are. For without that tameness, it would have been much more difficult for us to make any progress at all in learning their secrets. It would have been impossible to catch and individually colour-band every single bird in our study populations the way we do. Even if we could, it would have been futile afterwards to snowshoe through thick spruce attempting to find our newly banded jays, let alone observe details of their behaviour, if they always fled at our approach. And it would have been a hopeless fantasy to imagine that mated birds would lead us to their nests if we simply offered them appropriate nesting material, that we could count their eggs by using a finger to gently pry up an incubating female to peek underneath or, as happened once to an amazed student of ours, that an adult would come and feed a nestling in her hands while she was banding it.

No, even if we don't completely understand it, we have every reason to be personally thankful for the wonderful tameness of Canada Jays. And we have one more reason as well. Thousands of wide-eyed Canadian children, including our own, have had their first and most indelible first-hand connection with nature when a Canada Jay gently landed on their outstretched hand. A treasured memory for the rest of their lives. It doesn't get any cooler than that.

Does it harm Canada Jays to feed them?

Enticing a Canada Jay to the hand with a food offering is a pleasurable campsite or trailside activity, and many people trace their love of nature back to such experiences. But sometimes the worry is expressed that feeding Canada Jays bread, cheese, or raisins may distort their natural ecology, or even be unhealthy for them. It is true that such foods are "unnatural" and feeding large quantities to jays can indeed affect how well they do. Experiments we have conducted in Algonquin Park have shown quite clearly that providing winter food supplements causes breeding jays to raise more and healthier nestlings. Artificial feeding, in other words, brings about an ecological "distortion" alright, but one that most people would consider to be a "good thing", rather than a bad thing. As for the health question, it is well to keep in mind that Canada Jays normally subsist all winter on semi-rotten bits of raw, vertebrate flesh, insects, spiders, berries, and mushrooms, and all in various stages of decay, especially if there have been winter thaws (freezer failures) that encourage even more than the usual amount of bacterial growth. Given the questionable "healthiness" of these normal jay foods, we don't think you need to worry too much about doing harm when, from time to time, you share some cheese or raisins with a friendly Canada Jay that greets you on the trail.

— Dan Strickland and D. Ryan Norris

Gord Belyea

André Desrochers

André Desrochers

Jack Barclay

Marshall Drummond

Gord Belyea

Michael Runtz

CHAPTER EIGHT

THE NAMES OF THE CANADA JAY

Official Names. In North America, official scientific, English, and French bird names are adjudicated by a dedicated committee of what is now known as the American Ornithological Society or "AOS" (and before 2016 as the American Ornithologists' Union or "AOU").

"Canada Jay," restored as the official English name in 2018, goes back to at least the early 1800s. Before that, in the 1780s, two British ornithologists separately referred to our bird, described for the first time only a few years earlier in France, as the "Cinereous Crow" ("crow" no doubt being used in the British sense of designating any member of the diverse bird family known as the Corvidae). Sir John Franklin (yes, *that* Sir John Franklin) also used "Cinereous Crow" in an 1823 account of his first expedition to the Arctic in 1819–22. However, in a "Zoological Appendix" to the same work by Franklin, British naturalist Joseph Sabine used—to our knowledge, for the first time anywhere in print— "Canada Jay" instead.

Audubon and other, less well-known ornithologists were quick to adopt "Canada Jay" in the 1830s and '40s and, collectively, soon established it as the accepted English name of the species. This

Canada Jays remain together as a pair year-round (Dan Strickland) | Les Mésangeais du Canada restent en couple toute l'année. (Dan Strickland)

continued for over a century until the 1957 publication of the AOU's Fifth Checklist of North American birds. In that checklist, the then at least 134-year-old "Canada Jay" was replaced by "Gray Jay," a name originally coined in 1899 for an alleged subspecies of the Canada Jay confined to a relatively small range in the coastal mountains of British Columbia and the northwestern U.S. The reasons for elevating "Gray Jay" to become the overall species name in place of the well-established and much older name "Canada Jay" are somewhat complicated, and we refer readers wishing to know more to a 2017 article in the journal, *Ontario Birds*.[1] Suffice it to

[1] *"How the Canada Jay lost its name and why it matters"* by Dan Strickland, Ontario Birds, Volume 35 (2017), pages 1-16.

say here that the substitution of "Gray Jay" was defensible when first proposed in the 1940s but had lost its original justification by the time the 1957 checklist was published.

In fact, by using "Gray Jay' in its 1957 checklist, the AOU needlessly violated one of its own stated naming principles, namely that "traditional vernacular names should be retained whenever possible." When a group of mostly Canadian ornithologists pointed out this error in late 2017 and proposed that "Canada Jay" be restored as the official name, the AOS graciously agreed and formally announced the restoration, a few months later, in July 2018.

Vernacular Names. At least 30 English names have been used for the Canada Jay at one time or another, but by far the most common continues to be "whiskyjack." Used across Canada, and often the only name by which the bird is known to the general public, it is one of very few English vernacular names for a North American bird species borrowed from an Indigenous language and the only one that is widely used today. Its first known appearance in English (as "whiskerjack") was in a 1743 historical account of life at Hudson's Bay trading posts and, two decades later, another similar account said that fur traders around the bay were using both "whiskyjack" and "whiskyjohn." Despite appearances, these two names were not inspired by the Jack/John synonymy in English but, rather, were probably derived from two Cree words, *wîskicâhk* and *wîskacân*, both referring to the Canada Jay but in different dialects.

An understandable, but incorrect, link is often made by non-Indigenous writers between "whiskyjack" and the separate, albeit somewhat similar-sounding name, *Wisakedjak*. In Cree and other Algonquian cultures, *Wisakedjak* refers not to the Canada Jay but to a benevolent "culture hero, transformer, or trickster" (www.native-languages.org), who plays an important role in many traditional stories. But despite the apparent similarity of the two names, there is no more reason to think that the now English "whiskyjack" was derived from "*Wisakedjak*" than there is to think that whiskyjacks have anything to do with whisky. In both cases the similarity of the words is completely fortuitous and accidental.

Which is not to say that, given his magical powers and trickster proclivities, that *Wisakedjak* couldn't transform himself from time to time into an equally mischievous whiskyjack. Take a careful look the next time a Canada Jay lands on your hand!

French Names. The everyday colloquial name used in French-speaking Canada that more or less corresponds to "whiskyjack" is *"pie"* (feminine; pronounced "pee"). Used in New France at least as early as 1663, *"pie"* actually means "magpie" in French. Apparently the first French colonists, when they found a new and unfamiliar bird in the New World, gave it the name of the European bird it most resembled, if only distantly, and the name has stuck ever since. The official French name is *"le Mésangeai du Canada"*. *"Mésangeai"* (pronounced "may-zon-zhay") is a lovely name created by joining *mésange* (chickadee) with *geai* (jay). So, it might be translated as "Chickadee-jay" or even just "Chickajay".

Scientific Name. The scientific name of the Canada Jay is *Perisoreus canadensis*. "Canada" has always been part of the scientific name (as *"canadensis"*) right from the original description of the bird in 1760 by Mathurin Jacques Brisson, based on a specimen sent to Paris some years earlier from near present-day Québec City. The other part of the name, the generic *"Perisoreus,"* was coined in 1831 by a famous French-Italian ornithologist, Charles Lucien Bonaparte, a nephew of Napoleon. *Perisoreus* is a Latinized version of a classical Greek noun meaning "he who accumulates". So the scientific name of our bird translates into English as the "Canadian accumulator"—showing that Bonaparte was obviously well aware of the importance of food storage in the life and survival of the Canada Jay.

— **Dan Strickland**

CHAPTER NINE

AN INDIGENOUS VIEW: THE CANADA JAY AS RECONCILIATORY AGENT AND ENVIRONMENTAL EMISSARY—A MOST WORTHY NATIONAL BIRD

B eyond the inclusion of my drawing *For Seven Generations* in this book, which is an honour, I wish to begin by further acknowledging the desire of "Team Canada Jay" leadership to include contributions from all of Canada's three founding groups, and for reaching out to me to provide an Indigenous voice to the discussion at hand. So *miigwetch* to David Bird, the coordinating editor, and all my fellow co-authors!

As a point of respect, I want to first offer that I am acutely aware that the many First Nations spanning the country are exactly that, "many," and as such we are far from homogenous. Consequently, to speak for any or all of them would involve claiming a pan-cultural *right* to do so that I neither possess nor aspire to. In fact, in what follows I do not even claim to speak for the Nation to which I belong, the *Anishnabek*, nor the community of which I am a member, *Neyaashiinigmiing*. My offerings here, while informed by Indigenous values, are my own. As for my brief contribution, I want to go a little more broadly and deeply into the conversation and perhaps reach the reader on an *aspirational* level. I believe I am correct in saying that this book is ultimately intended to be more aspirational than informational—though it does indeed contain great information! In the previous chapter, for example, Dan Strickland capably addresses a couple of First Nations factual elements, so there is no need for trespass or repetition on my part. As an artist I am, as most artists are, far more interested in the transmission of new ideas or ways of looking at things, than in the communication of established facts. My fellow contributors represent an important range of disciplines and styles including, for example, the "whimsical" words of poet Colleen Archer, further enlivening our hopeful cause of having this particular *corvid*, the Canada Jay, named as the Country's national bird.

For what it is worth, I feel compelled to share that, as far as the bird's name goes, my own preference is that it be formally recognized by its more common and Indigenous-derived name, whiskyjack (see Chapter 8). That said, as the matter is now settled in that regard, I want to say that I am equally at ease with the name Canada Jay, for the simple reason that "Canada" is a variation of the Indigenous word *Kanata*, meaning "village." To my mind, this true meaning of the word only helps to further flesh out Number 12 on David Bird's list (see Chapter 4) of the 18 reasons the Canada Jay should be the emblematic bird for this "village" we call *Kanata/* Canada. So, let us not delay in making her our "village bird."

When I completed *For Seven Generations* in 2015, I decided to write an accompanying "story" that spoke to the threats posed by climate change—not only threats to the Canada Jay, but to all of us, and the collective responsibility we have to radically alter the way

The Canada Jay, cultural bridge-builder and symbol of environmental stewardship, *For Seven Generations*, by Anishinabek artist Mark Nadjiwan

For Seven Generations, par l'artiste anishinabé Mark Nadjiwan : le Mésangeai du Canada, créateur de ponts culturels et symbole de bonne gestion de l'environnement

Canada Jays are non-migratory and are well-adapted to survive and breed in our harsh Canadian winters (Marcel Gahbauer)

Les Mésangeais du Canada ne sont pas migrateurs et sont bien adaptés à survivre et à se reproduire dans nos rudes hivers canadiens (Marcel Gahbauer)

that we relate to the natural world for the sake of the *next* seven generations. I have continued this kind of messaging in both image and word in my more recent works as well (Dan Strickland and Ryan Norris also address environmental threats in Chapter 7). So to David's already compelling list of worthy reasons to make the Canada Jay our national bird, I would add that its role as an environmental messenger strengthens not only the case for such a designation (we are, after all, a big country with lots of environment to be concerned about!), but that such a designation could establish further common ground between settler Canadians and Indigenous Peoples.

As we know, the struggle to find common ground between our Peoples has been an enduring issue throughout the history of this land as we work toward a yet-to-be-fully-attained goal of truly becoming co-sovereigns, more equitably sharing a territory as per the original spirit and intent of the treaties. So, I would beseech all of us, Indigenous and non-Indigenous alike, to rally 'round the Canada Jay. To embrace her and her many fine qualities as our own, and to pay particular heed to her messages about re-envisaging the ways that we care for this land, for the sake of *all* those who dwell upon it. To be sure, though, this last request may understandably pose a challenge to more typical Indigenous values. Let me explain...

The practice among nation states of having a "national" animal, with its effect of raising one above all others, reflects a trait of many non-Indigenous cultures, where the status and integrity of the *individual* surpasses that of more *communal* interests and values. While it is certainly true that we Indigenous People have our Clan/Totem systems, headed up by animals whose attributes are to be brought to bear on one's own conduct, these systems pertain only to prescribed *roles*, and no one clan animal is ever elevated beyond the others in their importance. Let us not forget too, that conversely, some settler Canadians still embrace totemic remnants in their own societies (whether they know it or not!), as one needs only to think of service organizations like the *Lions* Club or the *Elks* Club. So, while an objection may well be raised against the goal of this book on the grounds that it runs afoul of "traditional" values, I would certainly respond by acknowledging the merits of those said values, while at the same time recognizing that *transformation* within any tradition is one of the most powerful! All cultures do and indeed *must* evolve and undergo change. Our People have, after all, already undergone perhaps more change than any other demographic in the country. And while most of that change has been thrust upon us, I believe that the aspiration of this book presents an opportunity for us to be active partners in change (rather than passive *recipients* of it), and to do so in the interest of the shared responsibility for environmental stewardship alluded to above. Thus, I am pleased to lend my Indigenous voice to such an act of further Reconciliation, though it be relatively small when compared to the much harder work that needs to be done ... all the more reason to take it up, perhaps.

Finally, the ongoing predicament on Mother Earth, including the ever-increasing threat of zoonotic diseases, is driven by the degradation of our natural environment—through human encroachment, wildlife exploitation, resource extraction, animal agriculture, climate change, and other stressors. I believe this reality bolsters the case for why parliamentarians should act to name the Canada Jay, a powerful winged environmental emissary, as the national bird. And as I have meandering thoughts about the current pandemic, I am struck by some curious wordplay that I suspect comes from afar. My home is on the Saugeen Peninsula, on Treaty 72 lands. Indeed, as I write these words by an open window facing north over a young cedar forest, I am sure that I hear whiskyjack in her alternate persona as Trickster, quipping from her home in northern Muskego, *"Jeez, them settler-government folks, ever tired of this COVID stuff, I bet ... maybe they need to talk about some CORVID instead, hehe ... do them some good, anyways!"* And as her mischievous giggle runs away with the next gust of wind, I know I can safely answer her on behalf of all the contributors to this book: "Ever hope so, us"!

— **Mark Nadjiwan**

This amazing mosaic floor in Murano glass and gold is an integral part of the Cathedral of the Transfiguration located in Markham, Ontario, and blessed by Pope John Paul 2 in 1984. The artwork and design for the mosaic were imagined by Fabrizio Travisanutto and Helen Roman-Barber, but the mosaic itself was fabricated and installed by Travisanutto Mosaics. The themes are the Militant Sheep, the Alpha and the Omega, the Celtic Cross, our Lord's fish, and for Canadian content, the Canada Jay

Cet extraordinaire plancher de mosaïque en verre de Murano entremêlé d'or se trouve dans la cathédrale de la Transfiguration, à Markham (Ontario), bénie par le pape Jean-Paul II en 1984. Cet œuvre a été conçue par Fabrizio Travisanutto et Helen Roman-Barber, et la mosaïque a été fabriquée et installée par Travisanutto Mosaics. Les thèmes en sont l'Agneau de Dieu, l'Alpha et l'Oméga, la Croix celtique, le poisson symbole de Notre-Seigneur, et pour le contenu canadien, le Mésangeai du Canada

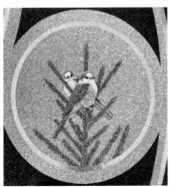

The Canada Jays featured in the mosaic tile floor created by Travisanutto Mosaics and Helen Roman-Barber were inspired by a photo by Dan Strickland featured on Page 58

Ces Mésangeais du Canada, représentés sur le plancher de mosaïque créé par Travisanutto Mosaics et Helen Roman-Barber, ont été inspirés par la photo de Dan Strickland présentée à la page 58

This Canada Jay makes its home in the boreal forest of Quebec (Rensje Duiven)

Ce Mésangeai du Canada vit dans la forêt boréale du Québec (Rensje Duiven)

CHAPTER TEN

LE MÉSANGEAI DU CANADA, UNE PRÉSENCE ANCIENNE DANS LA CULTURE FRANCOPHONE

L e Mésangeai du Canada fait partie de la famille des Corvidés (corneilles, corbeaux, pies et geais), qui sont peut-être les plus intelligents de tous les oiseaux. Il est étroitement associé aux forêts de conifères du Nord. Pas étonnant, alors, de le trouver en bon nombre dans la forêt boréale qui s'étend sur une très vaste portion du Canada. La forêt boréale couvre presque la moitié du territoire québécois, mais comme l'espèce visite aussi d'autres milieux, sa répartition totale englobe près de 75 pour cent du Québec.

Le Mésangeai du Canada, très résilient (comme beaucoup de Canadiens!), est bien adapté à vivre dans les régions froides et il peut même nicher à des températures de -30°C. L'oiseau réside ici toute l'année, et ne migre donc pas en hiver vers les pays chauds.

La première mention écrite de Mésangeai du Canada semble venir de Pierre Boucher, qui, dans son *Histoire véritable et naturelle*

des mœurs et productions du pays de la Nouvelle-France (1663), écrivait « Il y a des ... pies mais elles ne sont pas comme celles de France : car elles sont cendrées et mal-bâties ». Le jésuite Louis Nicolas, confirme ce fait dans son *Histoire naturelle* (vers 1700). Nicolas l'appelle *pie américaine* « pour ne savoir point d'autre nom d'un oiseau étranger qui ne ressemble du tout point à aucun des nôtres ». Dès les premières décennies de la colonie, le mésangeai a donc été appelé « pie », vocable populaire utilisé encore de nos jours.

L'oiseau a officiellement fait son entrée dans la classification scientifique en 1766, sous la plume de Carl Linné. Il est alors nommé *Corvus canadensis*, ce qui le place résolument dans ce qu'on appelle aujourd'hui les Corvidés. Linné avait appris l'existence de l'espèce dans l'*Ornithologie* de Jacques Brisson (1760)—un ouvrage monumental de plus de 4200 pages, qui a une place importante dans l'histoire de la discipline. Brisson y avait décrit le *Geay brun de Canada* d'après un spécimen de la collection privée du naturaliste parisien René-Antoine de Réaumur, dont il avait été l'assistant. Ce spécimen avait été expédié à Réaumur par Jean-François Gaultier, médecin du roi à Québec de 1742 à 1756. En 1831, l'ornithologue français Charles Lucien Bonaparte crée le genre latin *Perisoreus* (du grec περισωρεύω: emmagasiner), pour le *Corvus canadensis* de Linné et son proche parent européen, le *Corvus infaustus*. Étant admirateur et continuateur de l'œuvre d'Alexander Wilson (l'*American Ornithology*, 1808-1814), Bonaparte était bien au fait des mœurs de l'oiseau, et il y voyait une analogie avec les mésanges. Pour sa part, le nom générique français « mésangeai » est apparu peu après dans les *Compléments de Buffon* (1838), rédigés par René Lesson, qui y précise que l'analogie avec les mésanges est surtout dans la forme du bec et dans le comportement.

Au Canada français, on a longtemps calqué le nom américain de l'oiseau, *Canada Jay* (Geai du Canada)—changé en *Gray Jay* (Geai gris) en 1957 par l'American Ornithologists' Union. Le nom anglais a été ramené à *Canada Jay* en 2018, mais le nom scientifique reste toujours *Perisoreus canadensis*.

Geay brun de Canada

The first Canada Jay specimen (from near Quebec City) was depicted by the renowned French artist, François-Nicolas Martinet, in this painting that accompanied the first scientific description of the species by Mathurin Jacques Brisson in 1760. (Biodiversity Heritage Library)

Le premier spécimen du Mésangeai du Canada fut représenté par le célèbre artiste français, François-Nicolas Martinet, dans ce tableau qui accompagnait la première description scientifique de l'espèce par Mathurin Jacques Brisson en 1760. (Biodiversity Heritage Library)

Voici ce que James LeMoine disait de l'oiseau dans son *Ornithologie du Canada*, en 1861 : « En hiver, il se montre près des habitations sur la lisière des forêts, pille la cabane du voyageur et du chasseur* dans les bois, recueille les restes de pain ou de viande que ces derniers laissent après leur frugal repas, guette le moment ou le trappeur vient de tendre ses pièges, pour dérober l'appât.

*Cet oiseau est si peu défiant, que le chasseur le prend au moyen d'une attrape qu'il lui tend avec ses raquettes suspendues sur des petites branches. Il se construit un nid de branches et d'herbes sur les pins ... ; il vole par couple, emmagasine des fruits dans des arbres creux, et languit en captivité quoique son appétit continue d'être vorace : tels sont quelques-uns des caractères du Geai du Canada. En traversant la forêt l'hiver, on rencontre souvent ces oiseaux dans les sentiers battus, se posant à terre et faisant entendre un babil constant, sans marquer aucune défiance. Quand le cultivateur les voit, il conclut que la température va s'adoucir ou bien qu'une bordée de neige est imminente.»

Un siècle plus tard, dans *Les Oiseaux du Québec*, Raymond Cayouette (1972) décrit notre sujet à peu près dans les mêmes termes : « connu des bûcherons sous le nom populaire de *Pie* ... le feu du campeur ou du bûcheron attire invariablement cet oiseau peu farouche, qui vient sans gêne se servir dans les chaudrons. Il arrive d'ordinaire du sommet d'un arbre, plane silencieusement sur ses larges ailes et se glisse ainsi jusqu'au sol ou sur un arbre plus bas. Ce geai possède un répertoire étendu, comportant des jacassements déroutants, des sifflements doux et des imitations de cris d'oiseaux rapaces ».

Par sa répartition et son comportement, le Mésangeai du Canada est une composante bien ancrée du patrimoine québécois depuis le début de la colonie (et, évidemment, du patrimoine des Premières Nations bien avant la venue des Européens). Extrêmement familier envers les humains, le mésangeai a souvent été, au cours des siècles, le seul oiseau à visiter les nombreux trappeurs, explorateurs et colons autour de leurs campements, été comme hiver.

Cet oiseau, qui se retrouve en permanence dans toutes les provinces et territoires canadiens, représente certainement le meilleur choix comme oiseau emblème du pays ... et évoque parfaitement les Canadiens par son caractère amical!

— **Michel Gosselin et Alain Goulet**

TEN THINGS WE CANADIANS CAN DO

1) Buy this book and gift it to your friends, and even better, give a copy to your local federal Member of Parliament and any influential folks you might know;

2) Contact your local federal Member of Parliament by email, by telephone, or even better, in person and let them know that you want to see the Canada Jay officially recognized as our national bird as soon as possible;

3) Venture outdoors to your nearest boreal forest, whether it be a national or provincial park or a ski mountain, and seek out the Canada Jay to see how beautiful and friendly these birds truly are and to appreciate the magnificent habitat they live in;

4) Introduce your children and your grandchildren (or any children!) to the Canada Jay and do not forget to bring along your camera for a photograph they will never forget;

5) Make a donation to a favourite local, national and/or international organization that is committed to saving Canada's

Canada Jays do regularly frequent backyard feeders, provided they are located in appropriate habitat, e.g. in the Foothills of the Rocky Mountains close to Brown-Lowery Provincial Park (Kent Ladell *www.foothillsbirds.com*)

Les Mésangeais du Canada fréquentent régulièrement les mangeoires d'oiseaux à condition qu'elles soient dans un habitat favorable, comme ici dans les contreforts des Rocheuses, près du parc provincial Brown-Lowery. (Kent Ladell *www.foothillsbirds.com*)

boreal forest, conserving our birds, protecting our national and provincial parks, and/or fighting climate warming;

6) For those lucky enough to entertain Canada Jays at your backyard feeders, ensure that your feeders are clean and filled with fresh food and safe from window strikes and predation by cats, hawks and owls;

7) Visit the Canada Jay web site (www.canadajay.org) to sign the petition to be sent to the federal government, and if you are a celebrity or otherwise influential person, please consider taking it one step further and provide an endorsement quote to be placed on the website;

8) If you are a member of a stakeholder organization with strong roots in Canada, whether nature-related or not, convince your organization to write a letter of endorsement (see the website for a template if needed), which can be included on the website but also sent to federal politicians;

9) Use your local print and electronic media in whatever way you can, e.g. letter to a newspaper, phone call to a radio station, an article in a magazine, a blog or podcast on the internet, as well as social media, e.g. Facebook, Twitter, Instagram, etc., to promote the Canada Jay as our national bird;

10) And if you are a federal politician hopefully reading this book, whether representing the ruling party or not, please do everything in your political power to officially inaugurate the Canada Jay, truly the most Canadian bird, as our country's new national symbol.

This splendid oil painting of a Canada Jay family was done by Ontario artist Barry Kent-MacKay especially for the book (Barry Kent MacKay, see *www.barrykentmackay.ca* or *www.barry-mackay.pixels.com*)

Magnifique représentation d'une famille de Mésangeais du Canada, réalisée spécialement pour le présent ouvrage par l'artiste ontarien Barry Kent MacKay. (Barry Kent MacKay, *www.barrykentmackay.ca* ou *www.barry-mackay.pixels.com*)

ACKNOWLEDGEMENTS

In no order of importance, the authors would like to thank the following individuals for their help in publishing this promotional book on the Canada Jay. We are especially grateful to Robert Bateman and his two wonderful assistants, Alex Fischer and Kate Brotchie, for not only readily endorsing the bird with Bob's wonderfully moving "Foreword" but also for the one-time use of photos of his amazing paintings! Speaking of artwork, we cannot recognize enough Barry Kent-Mackay for doing a superb original painting of a family of Canada jays specifically for the book and with no small thanks to Dan Strickland's keen, experienced eye for detail on this species. We are equally fortunate to include two whimsical and colourful paintings of Canada Jays by Anne Hansen of Victoria, BC.

We must also acknowledge John and Janet Foster for their lovely tribute quote based on their field experiences with this tough little bird, not to mention the amazing photo contributions. Dan Strickland is particularly grateful to Michel Gosselin (Canadian Museum of Nature), Christian Artuso (Canadian Wildlife Service), and D.E. Pentland (University of Manitoba) for their helpful consultations in the preparation of his chapter on the various names of the Canada Jay. For the impeccably written French chapter (we truly wish that the whole book could have been in both languages!), we owe a heap of gratitude to Alain Goulet, Jean-Sébastien Guénette and Réal Bisson, Michel Gosselin, Maria Landry, and Daniel Mandron. Michel, Alain and Maria are particularly thanked for translating the captions. David Bird was especially pleased to receive the help of Mark Nadjiwan, a highly talented First Nations visual artist, who not only allowed us the use of his

Even on the coldest winter days Canada Jays have the wonderful ability to keep themselves warm—even their toes—by elevating their voluminous plumage. Very impressive for a bird that weighs just 65-75 grams! (Marcel Gahbauer)

Même lors des jours d'hiver les plus froids, les Mésangeais du Canada ont une merveilleuse capacité à se maintenir au chaud … jusqu'au bout des orteils, simplement en gonflant leur volumineux plumage. Impressionnant pour un oiseau qui ne pèse que de 65 à 75 grammes! (Marcel Gahbauer)

stunning drawing depicting a Canada Jay in the context of a traditional story from the Algonquin people, but also took on the task of penning a chapter on the bird from an Indigenous perspective, no easy task indeed!

Speaking of illustrations, no book on such a gorgeous creature would be complete without them. Patrick Lamontagne, a wickedly humorous political cartoonist, was very kind to let us use his highly appropriate cartoon in this volume. The book would simply not have been the same without the stunning photos of the Canada Jay taken by Dan Strickland, Ryan Norris and Amy Newman, Michael Runtz, Marcel Gahbauer, Gord Belyea, the Fosters, Kent Ladell, and several other kind individuals mentioned in various photo credits. Michael Runtz really went over the top with his incredible generosity in allowing us one-time use of his amazing photos of not only Canada Jays but also other appropriate species; please visit his Facebook and Instagram pages called *Nature by Runtz* for more. Helen Roman-Barber and Fabrizio Travisanutto are acknowledged for supplying the photos of the fantastic mosaic tile creation which includes a beautiful rendition of two perched Canada Jays and which graces the entranceway of the Cathedral of the Transfiguration just north of Toronto.

This book certainly would not have been possible without the generous financial contributions of both Alain Goulet, fellow author and president and owner of the retail store, 'Nature Expert' in Montreal, and Hancock House Publishers. Working with graphic designer, Jana Rade of Impact Studios in Kitchener, was a real pleasure! David Bird is also grateful to his wife, Toni, for her thoughtful insights into the book and for typing out the list of the names of national birds.

Last but certainly not least for the book itself, David Bird offers his heart-felt gratitude to our co-author and Poet-Laureate, Colleen Archer, for putting the initial spark of an idea for the book into his brain by revealing to him her whimsical poems on the official birds of our provinces and territories.

(Réjean Turgeon)

As for our cause in general, we must all tip our hats to Aaron Kylie and his staff at *Canadian Geographic* magazine and the Royal Canadian Geographical Society for initially running the contest and kickstarting what we hope will eventually be a successful venture! We must also be thankful to Chris Williams who took the initiative of creating and upgrading the *Change.org* petition, which has brought much attention and support to the cause. We also must acknowledge the enthusiasm and wise counsel of several politicians in seeking our objective, namely Dick Cannings (MP-NDP), Elizabeth May (MP-Green Party), Catherine McKenna (MP-Liberal), and David Johnston, David Bird's former hockey linemate at McGill University and Governor-General of Canada.

And finally, we cannot offer enough gratitude to Johanna Socha of Island Gals Media Group for donating her invaluable time and extensive web site expertise to create a highly attractive web site (www.Canadajay.org) dedicated to our cause!

A beautiful Canada Jay catching a few rays (Michael Runtz)

Ce beau Mésangeai du Canada prend une pause au soleil. (Michael Runtz)

The whimsical paintings of Victoria B.C. artist, Anne Hansen, frequently feature Canada Jays (*anitabike@gmail.com; oystercatchergirl.ca*)

Les peintures fantaisistes de l'artiste Anne Hansen, de Victoria (C. B.), montrent souvent des Mésangeais du Canada (anitabike@gmail.com; oystercatchergirl.ca)